HATE
WITHOUT A CAUSE

By Jam McNorton

Copyright © 2022 Jam McNorton
All rights Reserved
ISBN-13

Dedication

This book, Hate Without a Cause, is dedicated to my first born Kevin Anthony McNorton. Kevin passed away in 2020 due to a car accident.

Kevin, I wish that I would've gotten to know you. Unfortunately due to my personal problems of thugging and drugging I was never there for you. I take full responsibility for my mistakes. It was never on purpose.

Just as the truth is I was a bad father another truth, to me the only truth, is that I love you, and I always have and I always will.

Your father,

AKA Jam McNorton

Acknowledgements

First and foremost I acknowledge that God and all of his manifestations are paramount in my life. This is not a "Christian" book. This is a book written by a very sinful yet grateful "Christian." This expression of gratitude for my lord and savior "Jesus Christ" is personal and by no means has any bearing on the text of Hate Without a Cause in the realm of religion, conversion or any other way.

Thank you,
Jam McNorton

Thanks to My Support Team

The Laney Family - Motivation and Facilitators
Tom Stephan - Motivation
Jeff Dominguez - Editor
Chris Miller - Editor
Dr. Lorraine Abate - Typist
Rosie McNorton - Ear
Ed Cahoon - Manuscript Formatting

Table of Contents

Introduction ix
Chapter 1 The Monster 11
Chapter 2 White Superiority - The Lie 19
Chapter 3 The Supremacy Belief System 27
Chapter 4 Why Do Racist Whites Hate Blacks? 35
Chapter 5 Racial Hate: Removing the Veil 53
Chapter 6 Hate and Division: America's Destructive Path 61
Chapter 7 America's Law Enforcement: Justice or Just Us? 69
Chapter 8 Racist Whites: The "New" Slaves 79
Chapter 9 The "Ball & Chain Syndrome" 85
Chapter 10 Intra-Racism: Based on Nationality 93
Chapter 11 The Mirror 107
Chapter 12 The "New Generation" 113
Conclusion 119
Call to Action 123
Biography 125

Introduction

This book has been written to bring forth the truth about the reasons why some Whites hate Blacks. This book will also bring forth the truth that those reasons are invalid.

This is not a "blame Whites" book, although the facts about race relations between Whites and Blacks will be exposed in order to prove, or disprove, your beliefs about Black people in the area of human capabilities and human value.

This book was written to be an effective tool for racial healing, as well as a personal guide for racist White people to understand themselves and come to terms with the truth about why they hate Black people.

Finally, this book has been written with the hope of educating racist White people to understand that they do not have to continue hating Black people, because it is

HATE WITHOUT A CAUSE!

Chapter 1
The Monster

When I finally looked,
I finally saw,
the hate in me,
the lies they taught.
My hate though wrong,
I thought should be,
until I finally looked,
and I saw me.

- Jam McNorton

I am a citizen of the United States of America, the richest and most powerful country in the world, and I'm glad to be. I mean, heck, the United States of America (which I will refer to as simply "America" throughout the book) is well known as the "land of the free!" and the "home of the brave!"

"The land of the free?"

Well, in truth, it wasn't always like that, but that's another subject that we will cover later in the book. Let's get back to talking about my beautiful country "America."

America is a wonderful place to live and raise children, and it's a country where a person can literally arrive with very little, and with time, acquire a lot. There are many people in America who started their lives in poverty, but with hard work, a little luck and education, have become able to live the American dream (houses, cars, finance, etc.)

On the world stage, America is called a "Superpower" and it is for many good reasons. Economically we are the strongest, but our pass-out-the-cigars bragging right is the strength of our military. America's armed forces have been touted as the most powerful military on earth. Many enthusiasts claim that America has never lost a war. America has fought many wars, some for ourselves and some for our foreign allies. We are recognized as the "world protector." Now, as true as it may be about the fact that America has never lost a war (with the recent possible exception of Afghanistan) there is one other war that America has been fighting since before its inception and has never won.

"Come on…what war is that?" you ask. Okay, so this "war" I am speaking of is the longest war America has fought in its history. As a matter of fact, America has, as I said, been fighting this war since before it was actually a country, but the sad truth is that America is still fighting this war today, right here on our own soil. Usually when a war is being fought, there are two tangible sides, or combatants. Whether this is two countries, gangs, tribes, races, or two people, there is usually someone or something (as in the war on drugs) that can physically be seen, pursued, and dealt with, usually by force or fighting, as in the case of soldiers killing soldiers or by making arrests and getting drugs off the streets. Either way, by having a tangible enemy or combatant, the progress of the war can easily be assessed or measured.

So, why can't we defeat this enemy? We have the greatest military, the greatest minds, and the greatest resources, so what's the problem? Part of the answer is pretty simple: This enemy, this "Monster" is not tangible. It has no physical form. It has a name - it's called "Racism," but it is a belief, not a person. Don't get me wrong. "Racism" is a real enemy. It has all of the attributes of any formidable enemy. It has caused division among people. It has cost many innocent people their lives. It has caused many innocent Americans to be demeaned, demoralized, oppressed, and unfairly treated. It has caused racist White people to believe that humanistic value of Black people is equal to the beasts of the field.

Now that we have identified "who" the Monster (Racism) is, it's fair to say that we also need to know "what" the Monster (Racism) is. So let's find out.

According to Merriam-Webster's Dictionary, Racism is defined as:

1: a belief that race is a fundamental determinant

of human traits and capacities and that racial differences produce an inherent superiority of a particular race also: behavior or attitudes that reflect and foster this belief: racial discrimination or prejudice

2a: the systemic oppression of a racial group to the social, economic, and political advantage of another

2b: a political or social system founded on racism and designed to execute its principles

Note 2: "Racism."Merriam-Webster Dictionary
https://www.merriam-webster.com/dictionary/racism

The belief that race is a fundamental determinant of human traits and capacities, and that these racial differences produce an inherent superiority of a particular race is what? The White colonists who came to America truly believed that the "White race" was superior to all other races (sadly, many racist White people still share this belief today in America), so this racist belief caused the White settlers to engage with this "new" land with certain selfish objectives.

<u>Physical and psychological domination over all other races of people they encountered.</u>

Take all assets (land, valuables, positions of authority, etc.) Make all other races serve and fear White people, work for free, or be killed.

Money, gunpowder, and steel - "The White racist advantage"

"I know, let's take over the world!" As funny as that might sound, it was a real thought of the European White racists. This "thought" became the most successful mission in the history of mankind. Philip T. Hoffman, a Caltech professor, wrote a book published by the Princeton University Press in 2015 entitled "Why Did Europe Conquer the World?"

In Hoffman's book, he states that, although Europe only represents 8% of our planet's landmass excluding Antarctica, the Europeans colonized 84% of the planet from 1492 until 1914. Hoffman attributes the world domination success to one main factor: the Europeans advanced "gunpowder technology." Gunpowder and the European White racists' expert knowledge of the use of metals like steel, iron, and lead gave the racist White people the ultimate advantage. By combining these crafts, the White race was able to manufacture lethal weapons such as handguns, rifles, and cannons as well as shackles and chains. The colonists were also able to arm their ships. In these "new" lands embarked upon by the colonists, most of the natives had never seen nor experienced such weaponry. The question you may have is "What does this have to do with racism or Black people?" Keep reading, you'll see.

Jam McNorton

Supremacy - Pushing Hate

What did Black people do to merit all of the hateful treatment from racist White people? I mean, I can kind of understand anyone's desire to feel good about themselves. I also see that slavery was an economic advantage for the colonists.

What I fail to comprehend is where did the hate for Black people come from? I mean, the truth is that forced or not, Black people for the most part endured slavery. We tended to their fields, built and cleaned their homes. We took care of their kids, prepared their meals and whatever tasks we were handed. We stayed in our "place" when one of our loved ones was made to be an example by being publicly beaten or flogged to within inches of losing their life, or lynched for speaking to a racist White woman, or disobeying "Massah." Still, there is this undeserved hate for the Black race by racist White people, most of whom don't even have a viable reason for hating Black folk. Black slaves must have done such great work for the Southern states to have separated from the Union and called themselves a Confederacy. The Civil War was fought over the very Black people that racists today say they hate. I believe that much of the hate for Black people is due to unfounded reasoning and unjustified persuasion to fulfill the racists White people's belief that they are superior.

Fear Me, Serve Me, or Die!
(How the Black race became the mission)

In 1492 the European White racist landed in North America with their racist beliefs and gunpowder weapons to back up these beliefs. The first people that they encountered were Native American Indians. These people were dark-skinned, obviously of a different race, yet they were willing to accept the new European immigrants as co-existing neighbors for the most part as long as the immigrants respected the fact that "America" belonged to the Native Americans and also that they had their own beliefs and way of life and would not give up their beliefs or ways for anyone.

The Europeans had other plans, remember?
1. Dominate all other races.
2. Take everything.
3. Enslave the other races or kill them.

The Native American people are a very strong and proud race of people. This was their land and they weren't going to let the European White racist colonists just take away their home, only to be enslaved as a race without putting up a fight, so…the colonists had a big problem. Since they couldn't achieve their three superior goals to dominate, take, and enslave, they made a choice to eliminate all Indians that chose to resist their demands.

On August 20, 1619, a little over 20 Angolan slaves from off a slave ship were traded to settlers in the British colony of Virginia for some supplies. After using these slaves in Virginia, working them on the farms to accomplish whatever the settlers tasked the African slaves to do, the landowners realized that, unlike the Indians, these African slaves didn't fight back or argue, and they didn't have to pay them, 1, 2, 3! Thus, the North American slave trade was born.

Note 3: "African Americans at Jamestown" Historic Jamestown, Part of Colonial National Historical Park Virginia
https://www.nps.gov/jame/learn/historyculture/african-americans-at-jamestown.htm

It is common knowledge how Black people were treated during slavery, but what was it that the Black people did to be so hated?

Chapter 2
White Superiority - The Lie

"If it sounds to you like it sounds to me, it sounds just like a lie!"

-Mamie Lee Hillstock
(my mama, may she rest in heaven)

How long are racist White people going to push their superiority theory? Haven't we, as Black people, suffered enough from this unnecessary lie? Superior at what? This "superiority lie" is a total contradiction to our beloved Declaration of Independence, the second paragraph of which begins as follows:

"We hold these truths to be self-evident, that all men are created equal, that they are endowed by their Creator with certain unalienable Rights that among these are Life, Liberty, and the pursuit of Happiness."

Our forefathers wrote this, yet, as true as the words are, we as Black citizens of America have yet to see this passage fulfilled. This "superiority lie" has been haunting the Black race since the 1600's in America. But now the year is 2022, and it's time to address this superiority theory, and expose it as a lie.

Jam McNorton

Racist White people believe that White people are superior to all other races— especially the Black race, so, in order to explore this statement, I am going to ask some questions with regard to human capabilities and humanity. (These questions apply to people in America):

- Which race of people has endured unfounded hatred and mistreatment in America, Whites or Blacks?

- Which race has personally and systemically mistreated the other race, Whites or Blacks?

- Which race has never retaliated against the oppressing race for mistreatment, Whites or Blacks?

- Which race has helped to fight wars for the people that treated them worse than the enemies they helped to fight against, Whites or Blacks?

- Which race is still willing to forgive and love its oppressors, despite 400 years of abuse, systemically and personally, Whites or Blacks?

The following questions address capabilities (for superior racist Whites only):

- Are racist Whites the best at loving people, regardless of their color, race, gender, or economic status?

- Are racist Whites the best at admitting to themselves that hating people solely because of the color of their skin is wrong?

- Are racist Whites the best at hating people just because of the color of their skin?

- Are racist Whites the strongest at being able to stop hating people because of their color once they understand that the unfounded hate is wrong, regardless of what family or friends say or think about their choice to stop hating?

- Are racist Whites the best at standing up for America's principle that all men and women are created equal?

- Are racist Whites the best at asking themselves, "What has the race of people that I hate really done to deserve my hatred for them and then answering that question honestly?"

If you are wondering why these questions were chosen to determine superiority, it's because these are human qualities that truly reveal the character of a person. Book knowledge and physical attributes have nothing to do with the true measurement of human worth. It's one's ability to tear down misplaced walls and build useful bridges in their place, the ability to stop perpetuating unjustified, untrue, biased beliefs that only continue to promote division and mistreatment that reveals his/her true value to the rest of the world.

Where did this "Superior White Race" theory come from? No one can be sure how this belief came about, but there are a couple of "engines" that helped pass this lie on and dupe generations of impressionable White Americans into believing in its veracity. Amazingly, one group of racist persuaders of the White superiority theory was our "forefathers" themselves.

Before you get upset and throw this book out of the window, thinking that it is disrespectful to America's forefathers, realize that we are simply relaying truth. Any perceived disrespect that comes in truth is a deduction on the part of the reader.

Truth is the only way to fix what's broken in our great country.

<u>Engines of White Superiority - The Liars</u>

Would it surprise you to learn that most of the framers of our wonderful democracy -our "founding fathers" of America who wrote our bylaws such as the Constitution and our Declaration of Independence - were racist and slave owners?

The fact that our founding fathers were educated, prosperous, White slave owners, rather than ordinary, common citizens, is the reason their position on race mattered back then, and why it matters today in 2022. The problem is that the opinions of these powerful men, who just happened to be the architects of America's governmental bylaws, were not only heard, respected, and followed, but also obeyed. The opinions of the founding fathers were believed and ingrained in the hearts of virtually all of the White citizens of America back then, and their beliefs have transcended into what is called "rote learning" in the hearts and minds of many White people today.

Abraham Lincoln

Abraham Lincoln freed the slaves, but his position on "race relations" was different from his noble act of emancipation. In 1858, during a debate with Stephen Douglas for control of the Illinois General Assembly, Lincoln made this statement:

"There is a physical difference between the White and the Black races which I believe will forever forbid the two races living together on terms of social and political equality. And inasmuch as they cannot so live, while they do remain together, there must be the position of superior and inferior, and I, as much as any man, am in favor of having the superior position assigned to the White race."

Note 4: Lincoln, Abraham (2001). Collected Works of Abraham Lincoln. Volume 3. Ann Arbor, Michigan: University of Michigan Digital Library Production Services, pp. 145-202.

In the same speech, Lincoln also proclaimed:

"I will say then that I am not, nor ever have been in favor of bringing about in any way the social and political equality of the White and Black races."
See Note 4 above.

Abraham Lincoln made these immoral assertions without any certified tests or proof.

Sadly, the bigoted slander of Black people was not confined to the words of Abraham Lincoln.

Thomas Jefferson

In a 1785 publication called "Notes on the State of Virginia," Thomas Jefferson made these remarks of his position on race:

"I advance it, therefore, as a suspicion only, that the Blacks, whether originally a distinct race or made distinct by time or circumstances, are inferior to the Whites in the endowments of both body and mind."

Note 5: Jefferson, Thomas. Notes on the State of Virginia manuscript pg. 87, Thomas Jefferson Papers. Massachusetts Historical Society.
https://www.masshist.org/thomasjeffersonpapers/notes

Benjamin Franklin

In his 1751 Essay Franklin titled "Observations Concerning the Increase of Mankind," he made these remarks of his position on race:

"Why increase the sons of Africa by planting them in America, where we have so fair an opportunity, by excluding all Blacks and Tawnies, of increasing the lovely White and Red?"

Note 6: Franklin, Benjamin. National Archives Founders Online. Observations Concerning the Increase of Mankind.
https://founders.archive.gov/documents/Franklin

These remarks on race relations were made by our "founding fathers," the faces of Mount Rushmore. Of course, these quotes will stand up to the most rigorous fact checking.

There you have it, right from the most influential men in American history. White people have never been superior to Black people or any other race of people. This so-called "superiority theory," this fabrication, this lie, was promoted by men in power as a means of controlling subjugates out of fear of reprisals for the horrible mistreatment continually inflicted from the hands of Whites. Reprisals that Black people never planned or executed ever, even to this day.

The question we need to ask is, while White

superiority is one thing, what caused racist White people to hate Blacks? I really have been trying my best to wrap my head around this, but I still cannot come to grips with an adequate response. Is it justified or, HATE WITHOUT A CAUSE?

Chapter 3
The Supremacy Belief System

Chapter 2 examined "White Superiority – The Lie" and basically established that White people are not a superior race, nor is any other single race of people superior to any of the other races. In the quest to find some of the root causes for all of the social unrest in America today, the investigation has encountered an old, yet formidable, suspect. Oddly, this suspect has been able to hide within itself. I will explain how, but first, the explanation will make much more sense after a brief description of this suspect.

I call this suspect "Supremacy". Supremacy isn't a "who", it's a what. As a matter of fact this supremacy is a Belief. That's right! A non-tangible suspect, a very sly culprit in my view.

In case someone might be asking "what is this supremacy? I thought you said in the beginning of the book that was racism?"

Okay, well for those who wonder if, in fact, that this is the case and would like to know the difference between racism and supremacy, the explanation is clear.

Racism is the belief that one race of people is superior to another race or other races of people. Race is the key word in this definition. Racism is a belief of supremacy, but it's limited by its nomenclature. In other words, racism is the belief that one race is superior to others and, when the effects of racism, or actions from racism, are experienced, witnessed, or displayed, the results are negative.

The Supremacy Belief System on the other hand, while similar to racism in some ways, is a whole lot different in many others.

The reason supremacy is the suspect is because of its ability to hide within itself.

Unlike racism, which only produces negative results, "Supremacy" is actually a dual- purpose belief system. Supremacy is a belief system that has the ability to produce negative results, as with racism, yet (and here is the twist) this same belief system is used every day in society to produce positive results. People of all colors, races, creeds, genders, and transgenders currently use this belief system every day. We teach our players to believe that they are the best in their craft. Boxing trainers convince boxers that there is not a boxer on earth who can match their skills and abilities. Coaches ingrain the winning spirit into their teams to become the better team, to win. Teachers instill confidence in their students that their pursuit of education and knowledge will take them as far as their mind will allow. In these types of applications, the Supremacy Belief System produces positive results.

Trainers make champion boxers by teaching the Supremacy Belief System. Coaches win championships, etc. People excel in their individual career fields with the Supremacy Belief System.

This becomes the Positive Supremacy Belief teaching.

Beware of the "Double Edged Sword!"
Clearly, using the Supremacy Belief System can produce positive attitudes and results. It builds self-confidence, strength of mind, gratitude, and determination—all great qualities. It even makes the birds sing!

But there is another side of the Supremacy Belief System: the "Negative Supremacy Teachings." This is the core cause for most of the human relation problems in the world today, and it's powerful. The "you are better than others" teachings are similar to positive supremacy teachings, but that is where the similarities end.

Positive Supremacy Teachings

1. Positive Supremacy teaches a group of people or an individual that they are better than all other competitors.

2. Positive Supremacy is only taught for competition purposes (against others as in sports, academics, entertainment, etc.)

3. Positive Supremacy teaches the moral tools needed to be the best, including:

a. Respect
b. Honor
c. Integrity
d. Hard work
e. Humility
f. Gratitude
g. Generosity
h. Perseverance
i. Determination

4. Positive Supremacy teaches that the above moral tools must become part of the student's psychological "DNA" in and out of season, whether they are competing or not.

5. Positive Supremacy teaches that this "better than you" belief is only directed at competitors. Beyond that context, all students must honor the US Constitutional rights of all people, regardless of their race, color, gender, transgender, creed, or nationality. In other words, "leave it at the gym!"

Negative Supremacy Teachings

1. Negative Supremacy teaches a group of people or an individual that they are better than other people due to their race, color, creed,

gender or transgender. This Supremacy belief could be based on any one of a number of factors or a combination of differences, such as geographic location, education, income status, etc.

2. Negative Supremacy teaches people that they have rights that people who are not of the same status (race, gender, neighborhood, education, job, opportunities, etc.) shouldn't have. This concept is otherwise known as "privilege".

3. Negative Supremacy can be isolated, directed from one person to another (rivals).

To understand these two types of Supremacy Beliefs (positive and negative), see the following comparison chart illustrating the possible hypothetical social outcomes with positive and negative belief teachings in various sample belief applications.

Possible Results of Positive Supremacy Belief

Belief Teaching	Social Outcome
Teach boxer he is superior	Champion Boxer
Teach team they are better than all opponents	Win championship
Teach people that they are the most qualified applicant	Person lands the job
Teach someone that they are the best singer	Singer records an album

Possible Results of Negative Supremacy Belief

Belief Teaching	Social Outcome
Teach people they are superior because other races are inferior	Develops racist people
Teach gang members that other gang members are bad	Gang wars
Teach your children that their siblings are not as good	Sibling rivalry
Teach others that you are better than them WITHOUT A CAUSE	Low self-esteem, self hatred

Plainly put, Supremacy is a goal that many people strive for in many positive areas of life. Once achieved, supremacy allows a person or a group of people to experience feelings that are very pleasant to the mind such as, but not limited to:

1. Accomplishment
2. Completeness
3. Pride
4. Happiness
5. Worthiness
6. Acceptance
7. Fulfillment
8. Self-confidence

The problem is when this belief system is applied negatively. In other words, when people are taught to believe that other humans are lesser than them, no matter what the reason, whether race, gender, transgender, age, etc. They can't reconcile that, and to cover up the negative feelings, they act out in very negative ways.

No person on earth has the title of "better than other humans". A person may be better looking, have a better education, have a better job, have more money, have the means to travel and do things, but none of these advantages makes this person a better human.

Until people of all walks of life in America, especially people in power, understand the importance of the passage from our Declaration of Independence signed in 1776 which states that "all are created equal," America will continue to suffer from social unrest and inequality.

I truly believe in humanity. I also believe that we, as Americans, can defeat the products of Negative Supremacy Beliefs, specifically racism (personal and systemic). It is also my belief that in order to defeat these enemies, it will take all of us. Anyone wishing to join the fight against the products of Negative Supremacy Beliefs should answer one two-part question to receive some valuable insight. This question is for EVERYONE:

Question: Do I believe that I am better at doing things than others? OR Do I believe that I am better than others?

Chapter 4
Why Do Racist Whites Hate Blacks?

"Hey man, you're alright! But I still hate Niggers."

It was sometime in the middle of the summer of 1983. I was in the Air Force and stationed in Sacramento, California. 1849th Engineering Installation Squadron (EIS) was my unit, and we were tasked with installing communication systems in different parts of the world. I had been in the unit for less than a year, and the only place they had sent me was San Antonio, Texas, and all that job really entailed was building some communication cabinets. They were going to be shipped out, so I really didn't get to experience a real installation job.

But the next job was the big one that we all had been waiting for, four months at Clark Air Base, Philippines temporary duty: h-e-a-v-e-n! Girls, bars, and more girls and more bars... It was a big radio installation job, so big that two teams were needed to complete the project. In response, our unit sent ten of our military personnel, along with our civilian boss, Bob (he was the best), to meet another team from Yokota Air Base, Japan.

The morning after arriving in Manila, we drove

out to Clark Air Base, where we checked into temporary lodging. Because there is a 16-hour time difference between California and the Philippines, I went straight to sleep.

The next morning, I got up and walked outside, and all I could say was "Wow." I saw banana trees, and for a minute I thought I had died and gone to heaven. It was beautiful. I had been told about the Philippines, but I had no idea until I stepped outside how beautiful it actually was.

The next day, both teams met up at the communication squadron for our initial briefing. Carl, Steve, Tennant, and I walked into the Com Center with our boss, Bob (the only civilian on the job), and the rest of our guys, who were antenna guys. We were radio jocks, so the other guys were out in the field. We walked into a big empty room, where a Master Sargent was standing in front of a podium speaking to the team from Yokota Air Base. I presumed that he was the team leader, and, of course, we were late from going out bar-hopping the night before. As we expected, he ribbed us, but he was gentle, kind of.

"Heyyy…Fellas! I am so glad y'all could join us. I hope that we didn't disturb you fellas! Bob told me that y'all got yourselves acquainted with the "ville" last night and tied one on and that's okay, but you goin' to have to save the partyin' for the weekend. I don't know what y'all do in California, but me and my boys are from Yokota, and we work! And we show up on time! This is a big job, and we've only got four months to do it, understand?"

"Yes sir!"

After a few hours of debriefing, the Master Sargent said, "Alright, well we're going to take a 30-minute break because Bob and I need to go over some things. Now there's lunch in the break room. This will give both teams a chance to meet. Let's meet back in here at 1300 (1:00 PM), okay?"

"Yes sir!"

We all headed to the break room to eat and greet. There was a lot of good food, and I found out that some guys knew each other from other bases. Other than the guys on my team, I didn't know anyone, so after I devoured my lunch, I started walking around the room to meet the other team members. After shaking hands with three or four guys, I saw some skinny young White kid sitting at a table with some other White guys. I noticed that they weren't trying to meet anyone, like they were isolated in their own world. I walked up to them and stuck out my hand and said,

"What's up guys? I'm Keith."

None of the three shook my hand. They looked at each other and laughed. I said, "I don't know what's so funny, but I'm Keith, who are you guys?"

The skinny kid I noticed first answered, "Yeah, we gotta work together, but I'm gon' tell you right up front, I'm from Georgia, and, where I come from, we don't like Niggers!"

I didn't expect that. It was like I was in suspended animation - everything just stopped for about five seconds, as though I were in The Matrix. When I finally snapped back into consciousness, I don't know how or why, but I looked at him and said, "That's okay, what's your name?"

Oddly, he told me that his name was Victor, but it was the way that he looked away after he told me his name. I could see his pain, so I just told him that I was glad to meet him and walked away.

Victor didn't work with me during the four months, but he got to work with my new best friend Carl. They worked at the transmitter site, and I worked at the receiver site. Outside of Clark Air Base was the "Ville," a whole lot of bars with a whole lot of girls. We all hit the bars on the weekend. The Yokota team hung out with their own team, and so did we. One night, Carl and I were walking down a little dirt road that had a lot of the main bars and food and such. Steve was with us, and he asked Carl and me if we could stop at the "Viking" bar, where they played rock 'n roll and catered to everyone, but mostly White service members hung out there. When we stepped into the joint, of course there were a lot of military (mainly White), loud rock 'n roll, girls dancing on platforms, guys wearing Viking helmets with horns on them. It was a typical Friday night bar scene in the "Ville." The Viking bar was a small bar, and it was packed. As we started a walk-thru, in the back of the club I saw two guys standing over a table fussing at a third young man. As we got closer, I saw that the third man was Victor, the kid from Georgia. He was with his two cronies.

Victor was trashed, and as we got close enough, I could see that his friends were cussing him out for being drunk off his ass. I stepped up to the table and asked his friends, "What's up? What's wrong?"

One of the guys turned to me with a look as though I had sinned for speaking to him. He replied, "Fuck him, I ain't baby sittin' this asshole!" Then he and his friend turned and walked out of the bar.

After Victor's friends left, I asked him if he was all right. He replied, "Heyyy, McNorton and Carl...you know...the truth is...y'all the only Niggers that's alright, 'cause you know I hate Niggers, but you and Carl, y'all alright man!"

Then he fell off of his stool. Carl and I picked him up, and once we got him on his feet, we each grabbed an arm and walked him out of the bar. When we got him outside, I said to Carl and Steve, "Hey you guys, he's fucked up. We can't leave him like this. We gotta get him back on base!"

Steve said that he had to meet a girl at another club, so I volunteered to take him back. After Carl and Steve left us, I hailed a trike, (a motorcycle with a side car), and we took off for the main gate. I got him out of the trike, paid the driver, threw his arm over my shoulder, and walked up to the gate. The guards were cool, and one helped me to get Victor into a base taxi. Both teams were housed in trailers, so I took Victor to the trailer where Carl and I lived and dumped him on the couch.

The next day was Sunday, so I cooked breakfast - pork chops smothered in milk gravy, grits, scrambled eggs with onions and cheese, bacon, and biscuits.

"Come and get it! Carl, wake Victor, up!"

Carl and the two Filipino women who had come back with us from the club ran toward me and the kitchen. Carl stopped on the way to the food and shook Victor. Victor woke up swinging like he didn't know where he was.

"What the fuck!" he said.

"Hey, slow down o' country-ass boy!" I replied. "You all right. Your so-called friends ran off and left you at the Viking bar around 10:00 last night. You was fucked up! But we couldn't leave you like that, so I brought you here. Now, get your ass up and go put some water on your face and come eat."

The next ten seconds were truly an epiphany that the whole room vicariously shared through this young man. The reality of where he was, who he was with, the events of last night that caused him to be here, and the betrayal of his friends had slowly dawned on him. The beauty of the realization danced in his eyes for all of us to see, when it occurred to him that his most vulnerable moment maybe in life was met with empathy and compassion from the race of people he swore he hated.

Reality serves irony humble pie.
-Jam McNorton

Everyone started eating, and the food must've been pretty good, 'cause all you could hear were forks hitting plates.

"Man, I ain't had none of this since I left Georgia!" Victor said after he burped from the Old English 800 he was drinking with breakfast.

When everyone was finished eating, one of the girls did the dishes. After a good cigarette, Victor walked to the front door and turned to

Carl and me sitting on the couch. He completed the epiphany with his head tilted and his humble eyes looking at the ground he quietly said, "Thanks man."

Then he left.

After a considerable amount of more work, the job finally came to the end, and, on the last day, both teams gathered at the receiver site for our briefing. When the briefing was over, as we were saying our goodbyes, Victor walked up to me and said, "Hey man, you're alright, but I still hate Niggers."

He laughed and stuck his hand out. I grabbed his hand and pulled him to me, and, as I patted his back, I whispered in his ear,

"You're alright too, V. Love you man."

We left, and, after a long flight back to California, just as we were landing, a thought flooded my mind that maybe, just maybe, Carl and I were sent to the Philippines for more than one job!

There are so many stories of racial indifference that don't end like this one did. It's a shame, and the sad truth is that America has been suffering from this type of unfounded hate for too long.

I have asked quite a few White racists why they hate Black people, including the young man

Victor from the Air Force, and what I have found is that all of the racist White people that I have asked either gave me a dumb, untrue answer like, "Black people are no-good" or "Black people ain't the same as White people."

Other answers to the question, to me, were more truthful, such as, "I don't know, it's always been that way all my life. My whole family and most of my friends hate Nig—Black folk. Y'all just need to go on back to Africa and leave us good White folk alone!"

The best and most truthful answer I ever heard was, "I don't know why. That's how I was raised, and I just do!"

This is the reason! Childhood conditioning. We share the religion, the politics and the racial attitudes of our parents.

Let me be clear on why racial hate is so important to this author, thus the reason I chose to write this book. My reason is very simple: The unfair, unfounded, personal, group and systemic hate that White racists have toward Blacks has gone on for too long. It hasn't been 400 seconds, minutes, hours, days, weeks, or months. This White racist hate for Blacks has been going on for over 400 years.

<u>Black Wall Street</u>
<u>100 years later: No Justification, No Reparations</u>

Until recently, most people in America had never heard of Black Wall Street, the most prosperous "Black Owned" business district in America during the early 1900's. This historical phenomenon got its birth in Tulsa, Oklahoma. Between 1865 and 1920 many "freed" Black people migrated to Oklahoma in search of a better life. Tulsa had oil money and the Klu, Klux, Klan which made the city very segregated.

This meant that most Blacks would have to take menial service jobs (janitor, porter, maid, etc...). Undaunted by the reality of "Jim Crow" laws for Black Americans, the spirit of determination to succeed in business as a whole community stirred in the hearts of the Black citizens of Tulsa. They were convinced that all they needed was leadership and the means.

As a sign from above, both leadership and the financial means sprang forth in the forms of two Black entrepreneurs: O.W. Gurley and J. B. Stradford. Mr. Gurley bought 40 acres of land in Tulsa, naming the land Greenwood after a town in Mississippi. In 1906, O.W. Gurley opened the first "Black-Owned" business in Greenwood, a boarding house for Black Americans. J.B. Stradford built the biggest "Black Owned" hotel in America, the 55 room hotel called "The Stradford" after its namesake.

Both men understood the historical plight of the Black American from the exploitation of slavery to the Jim Crow laws of the early 1900's. These

Jim Crow laws disfavored Blacks in many areas including jobs, housing, voting, and education. As a simple but telling example Blacks were required to enter establishments from only back entrances while Whites entered via the front door.

O.W. Gurley and J. B. Stradford shared a vision of success for all of the citizens in the Greenwood neighborhood. The goal was to create a financially self-sustaining community, a community built and owned by Black Americans. It this Author's opinion the reason for such an ambitious goal was to rise above the oppressive existence afforded to Blacks by racist Whites.

According to articles published in the New York Times, Wall Street Journal, and History.com, both men believed that in order to reach the goal of community self- reliance, they would have to help those who desired to start a business in Greenwood with start-up costs, so that's exactly what they did. Mr. Stradford also believed in the importance of the community "pooling" their money together. It has been said that all of the income would circulate through Greenwood many times over before leaving the neighborhood.

From 1906 until 1921, Greenwood, the little Black neighborhood located on the north end of Tulsa, accomplished unprecedented financial feats as a community. The neighborhood did more than survived, it thrived. The community opened over 70 successful businesses in 15years.

The Greenwood neighborhood became the "Greenwood District" thus this Black-Owned successful Business District became known as "Black Wall Street" to all of America. Most Black citizens in the community had big houses, new cars and all without any White input.

Now, supposedly, these Black Americans weren't smart enough to do much of anything without the guidance of the more intelligent White man. Well, the truth is, according to historians, these inferior Black Americans not only accumulated wealth, they had their own banking system, post office and even their own schools. To this Author, Black Wall Street proved that all men are created equal.

So why didn't this Black Wall Street survive? It wasn't because of any shortcomings in the Black community. Instead, as a result of a mix of White racist hate and fear, the burgeoning Greenwood community was subjected to an onslaught of burn, kill, and cover. I wish that I had a happy ending for the citizens of Greenwood. It would be my pleasure to continue describing their success, but sadly and regrettably, as fate would have it, this once thriving suburb of Tulsa, along with its prosperous potential for the future, came to an abrupt end.

The end, the end, the end!!! The reason I chose to describe Black Wall Street was not to tout its success, but to remind us of the abrupt ending of this Black American Success.

On May 30 1921, a young Black man named Dick Rowland entered the Drexel building in the "White" Business District of Tulsa. Mr. Rowland chose to take an elevator. Unfortunately (according to all the many various sources I have read…History.com, NYT) the young Black man lost his footing while he was entering the elevator and stumbled. As he attempted to grab onto something to prevent himself from falling, his hand grabbed the shoulder of a 17 year old White girl named Sara Page. Ms. Page was the Elevator Operator. The young lady screamed and Dick Rowland ran.

On May 31, 1921 Dick Rowland was arrested for sexual assault (History.com "The Tulsa Race Massacre"). The White newspaper carried a story of the lynching of Dick Rowland, a 19 year old Black man accused of sexual assault on the 17 year old White Elevator Operator Sara Page.

Although Ms. Page refused to press charges, a White mob gathered outside the jail where Dick Rowland was being held, demanding the Sherriff to hand Rowland over. The Sherriff refused. Later, approximately 75 armed Blacks posted outside the jail to protect Rowland. They were met by a mob of over 1,000 protesting White

men, including many who had been deputized by City officials (History.com 2020). Then starting before midnight, thousands more Whites converged onto Greenwood, killing Blacks, burning down virtually all of the Black Owned businesses and over 1,200 homes. Another 200 homes were not burned, but looted instead. It was reported that when the Fire Department tried to put out the fires, the White mob threatened their lives. It was also reported that dynamite was dropped on the Greenwood District from airplanes.
(History.com).

Finally, the Governor of Oklahoma declared Marshall Law at 5:00 pm the following day on June 1 and brought in the National Guard. For decades there has been controversy over how many Black people were killed. The Tulsa Historical Society reported a total of 36 dead (10 Whites and 26 Blacks). Most historians cite the number of Blacks killed to be between 100-300 (NYT, History.com).

The National Guard put out the fires in homes and businesses and built Internment Camps in accordance with Marshall Law. The burning of over 1,200 homes displaced an estimated 6 to 8 thousand Black Americans. To add insult to injury, these same 6 to 8 thousand Black Citizens of Greenwood were arrested for unlawfully rioting and put into the Internment Camps.

On June 2, 1921 Dick Rowland had all charges

dismissed. It was reported that he left town and never returned. What took Greenwood citizens 15 years to build, the White mob destroyed in less than 24 hours – 35 city blocks burnt down (History.com).

According to historians (NYT, History.com) this was one of the most horrific race massacres in American history and until recently, in 2022, has received very little press. In the days following the massacre, the White newspaper "The Tulsa Tribune" removed the May 31, 1921 front page story about lynching Dick Rowland (History.com).

The Tulsa police and state Militia records disappeared as well.

The Tulsa Race Massacre was not added to the Federal History Schoolbook Curriculum until 2009. The blame for the massacre, first called a riot, was assigned to Black Tulsans. Not one White Tulsan has ever been charged with murder. The

Race Massacre has never been addressed by Tulsa government authorities. There have never been reparations to the Black community or their descendants for property damages and seizures and more egregiously never for the Black lives lost.

Now that we know this much about Black Wall Street it's important that we ask questions.

Questions that for 100 years have not been answered by any accounts of this despicable display of racism in its purest form.

1. Did the Tulsa Race Massacre of 1921 just happen or was it planned?

2. Was Dick Rowland a victim or a participant?

3. If the goal of the White mob was to lynch Rowland, why didn't they burn down the jail and kill him and let it be done?

4. History. Com stated in their article (Tulsa Race Massacre 2018) that there was rumor of an insurrection by the Black Tulsans, but why would those residents from Greenwood do that when they lived as well or better than the White racists who perpetrated the Massacre?

5. Did the Tulsa Race Massacre happen out of racist hate, fear, or both?

6. If out of fear, what fear? Was it the fear that the success of this Black community would be the template for Black people all over America?

7. How many White participants were ever arrested and convicted of murder?

8. If the mob members were in fact deputized as reported, wouldn't this make Tulsa and the state of Oklahoma liable for the killings and

property damage sustained by Greenwood citizens?

9. Why was this story buried for so long?

10. Is our Federal Government finally going to make reparations for the citizens of Greenwood?

11. Murder has no statute of limitations, so are the murderers of Greenwood going to be brought to justice?

12. If dynamite was in fact dropped on Greenwood, how could Tulsa not know who flew the airplanes?

13. With Jim Crow laws in effect in 1921, how could Dick Rowland even ride on an elevator with a White person?

14. What did the burning of up to 35 square blocks of Greenwood and killing upwards of 300 Black residents have to do with Dick Rowland and what he was accused of?

The bottom line is what was done to this community is one of the worst displays of White hate and fear of Black people in our American history. For 100 years, Tulsa has not made any attempts to "right the terrible wrong". There haven't been any public apologies, justifications or reparations for the citizens of Greenwood and their dependents. The fact that the truth is finally emerging is progress.

Jam McNorton

There are so many stories of racial difference that don't end like this one did. It's a shame, and the sad truth is that America has been suffering from this type of unfounded hate for too long.

Chapter 5
Racial Hate:
Removing the Veil

"And the truth shall set you free"
--The Bible, John 8:32

Today in the news, our top story comes to us from Charlottesville, Virginia. "White supremacist and White nationalist groups marched by the hundreds with torches and weapons in hand to hold a racist rally in Charlottesville last night. The White racist groups were met by anti-racist folk, and a standoff ensued. Quickly, the standoff became violent, and many of our sources on the ground tell us that law enforcement did nothing to stop the fighting. At the conclusion of the rally, one person - a female - had been killed."

[Clock ticking] "Tick, Tick, Tick, Tick..."

Many "glass half empty" pessimists believe that events such as this rally in Virginia are part of a racial time bomb that will eventually start the biggest race war between Whites and Blacks. Contrary to their negative thinking, I, being of the "glass half full" persuasion, see events such as Charlottesville in a much different manner.

(My condolences to the family of the young lady who died.)

See, somewhere in my Holy Bible, God says, "That they meant bad for you, I will make good for you, whose eyes stay on me."

I might be paraphrasing here, but what the scripture is saying to me is a couple of things:

1. The pessimists are focusing on the wrong parts of the confrontation. The pessimists keep focusing on the "aggressors" with torches and weapons. "New" White people are suffering from the very "old" disease called racism. A curable disease by which Black Americans have been victimized for over 400 years. (This is the "That they meant bad for you" part.)

2. The pessimists would have a strong chance of beholding the same glass as "half full" and have all the hope and increased faith in humanity if they would take the time to notice that the anti-racist folks stand in solidarity with people from all races, colors, creeds, genders, transgenders, and ages. Thanks to the social media and cellular phone companies, the pessimists will see that "change" is not just coming for America, but the solidarity of anti-racist folk being demonstrated in every country in the world proves that "change" for world-wide race relations is here! (This is the "I will make good for you" part.)

I wish that the solidarity around the world for

different races was the part where we could start rolling the credits—racial hate solved. But the truth is that as wonderful as the anti-racist togetherness is, this is only one side of the equation. We still have a lot of work to do to free our fellow humans from the bondage of being racist without a cause!

Now back to this "racial hate" thing, specifically hate for Black people from racist Whites. It's time to remove the veil and find out just what Black people have done to White people to merit all this hate.

The chart on the next two pages describes the known aggressions of Black people toward Whites, from slavery through 2020. This comparative chart of aggressions further describes White people's aggressions toward Blacks, from slavery through 2020. The aggressions used for this comparative chart are based on recorded facts only.

Jam McNorton

Racial Mistreatment Comparative Chart: Whites vs. Blacks

Blacks' Mistreatment of Whites	Time Period	Whites' Mistreatment of Blacks
N/A	1600-1800	Slavery - forced labor, beatings, lynchings, treated Blacks like cattle, branded Blacks, no education for Blacks
N/A	1865-1910	Southern Code laws for freed Blacks—no rights to vote or own land. Segregation, separate justice for Blacks. Supreme Court upholds segregation laws—worse education for Blacks.
N/A	1920	Jim Crow Laws and segregation
N/A	1921	Tulsa, OK Race Massacre/Black Wall Street and Greenwood District businesses and homes burned. Blacks

		slaughtered
N/A	1930-70's	Redlining Black neighborhoods. High interest loans or no loans. Housing segregation.
Passive resistance protests in order to improve civil rights, sit-ins (peaceful), and civil rights marches.	1960's	Separate dining, bathrooms, etc. Black men could receive death penalty for insulting White women or be publicly flogged. Hoses turned onto Black civil rights activists, dogs allowed to bite Black protesters, Blacks jailed for peaceful civil rights protests.
N/A	1994	Unfair crime bill locking up Black men.
N/A	2008	Reverse redlining—bad home loans for Blacks causing Black foreclosures.
N/A	2014-2020	White racist cops killing unarmed Blacks.

This chart (easily fact-checked) is intended to bring some enlightenment and help to remove the veil of the decades of lies and unfounded reasoning and justification for hating Black people. This chart is to make the fact clear that, if your reasons for hating Black people have been predicated on our mistreatment of White people as a whole, then it's time that the veil were removed and replaced with the truth. The truth is that, for over 400 years, Black people have been used and abused by White people, and Black people have never retaliated or even had the thought of doing so. Yet, they are still vilified? Black people have been enslaved, denied access to the best education, jobs, and opportunities, forced to use separate bathrooms and water fountains, and made to ride at the back of the bus. The truth is that no matter what has been done to Black people, the mistreatment could not break them. The unfounded hate of many Whites has never stopped Black people from standing and rising as Americans.

If racist Whites or anyone would look at these mistreatment charts, they would have to agree (if they would decide honestly) that Black people as a whole have not mistreated Whites, and therefore if hatred of Blacks is based on how Blacks have treated Whites, then your justification for hating Blacks is baseless. In order to illustrate this point, a few important facts need to be brought out:

• Blacks have never desired to mistreat White people, even after all of the mistreatment that they, as a race, have had to endure from Whites.
• Black people have never had the power or

authoritative positions (government, law enforcement) to facilitate such immoralities.
- Black people as a whole do not hate White people - there are Blacks who do not trust White people, but they do not hate whites.
- Black people are not in competition with White people, nor are they your enemy. All they desire and demand is their civil rights as Americans.

It is anyone's right to choose who or what they like or don't like. It is also anyone's right to choose who or what they love or hate. It doesn't matter how they came about their decision. If racist White people hate Black people, it is their right. What racist White people don't have the right to do is to let their decision to hate Black Americans violate Black folks' inalienable right to life, liberty, and the pursuit of happiness, as guaranteed to all Americans.

If there were any justification for one race to hate another (and there's not), wouldn't it be true to say that from a moral perspective, Blacks truly have many more fact-based reasons to hate White racists? We don't hate you, we as Black folk, after 400 years of unfounded mistreatment from racist Whites simply want the personal or systemic racial hate and mistreatment to stop! Racist Whites have hated Blacks for too long, so I challenge all of my readers to answer this question honestly: Is the White racist mistreatment of Black Americans justified or HATE WITHOUT A CAUSE?

Jam McNorton

Chapter 6
Hate and Division: America's Destructive Path

"United We Stand, Divided We Fall!"
--John Dickinson, "The Liberty Song"
(First published on July 7, 1768, in the Pennsylvania Journal and Pennsylvania Gazette newspapers)

In earlier chapters, a very important issue was addressed: the hate for Blacks by racist Whites. It's sad to say that America's problems are much bigger than the racial divide between these two groups, and I believe that there are two words that are paramount causes for many of America's social inequities. These social inequities include, but are not limited to: race relations, education, jobs, pay inequities for race and gender, housing, and many more... The two words I'm speaking of are HATE and DIVISION. I believe that if hate and division are not addressed with more than just a conversation, they could very well become "the road to destruction" for American Democracy as we know it today.

Jam McNorton

Politics and Lies = Hate Gone Wild!

Let's be clear, I said "hate and division" not "hate and diversity". Diversity is great! It gives us choices. "Division" is, well, divisive. I'm not speaking of Division as a military unit capable of standing on its own to complete missions for our country.

No, I'm speaking of the Division that comes from the root word "Divide". Division means to separate the whole and usually means that the separate sides have different views and, typically, (as with Democrats and Republicans) rarely come to a shared or bipartisan agreement. The Division in America is much bigger than the racial divide, but I believe racism, along with politics, are two of the most persuasive templates or models of the Division problem in America.

In case anyone has doubts about how powerful and persuasive words can be, especially untrue, baseless lies, I hope that the events that occurred at our Nation's Capital on January 6, 2021, as well as the events that preceded what happened at the Capitol that day, will bring clarity to the eyes and ears of everyone regarding the power that persuasive lies can actually have over a group of people

January 6, 2021

The following is simply a summation of the

events that occurred on this day.

Normally, a political day such as January 6, 2021, would not draw any major media attention. I mean, after all, the 2020 election was over, and January 6, 2021, was simply chosen as a day to confirm the voting choices of the Electoral College, our protocol for selecting our nations' leader, the President of the United States, for the next four-year term. It's called a Democracy, remember?

For whatever reason, protocol or not, "simple" just wasn't in the cards on this day as far as America's "Democratic electoral process" was concerned.

According to reports by all of the major Newspapers and News Networks (Wall Street Journal, New York Times, ABC, NBC, and CBS, to name a few), Congress was to convene in a joint session at approximately 1:00pm EST on Capitol Hill to certify President Elect Joe Biden as the 46th President of the United States of America.

Unbeknownst to our congressional leaders, there was a collaborative storm brewing outside, comprised of political deception and far-right-wing racist hate, the strength of which was almost unimaginable.

Apparently, President Trump in the last days of his term refused to accept the results of the 2020

Presidential election, results that mandated President Trump to be replaced by President-Elect Biden. As a matter of fact, according to Wikipedia, after the election, the Trump campaign, along with other groups in support of Mr. Trump, filed over 60 lawsuits in hopes of overturning the results. The suits ranged from contesting election processes to vote counting, as well as the vote certification process, in multiple states. Most suits were dismissed for lack of evidence. The courts said the lawsuits were frivolous and without merit (Wikipedia). Mr. Trump refused to concede, asserting widespread voter fraud in public statements, but the assertions were rarely made in actual court proceedings (WSJ, NY Times, 2021).

On January 6, 2021, in defiance to the Electoral College voting certification proceedings on Capitol Hill, President Trump held a "Save America" rally on the south side of the White House. President Trump started his speech around noon. He had thousands of supporters at his rally and hundreds of supporters gathering on the west side of the Capitol.

The President started his speech in pure uncensored Trump style, pushing his false narrative of how he was robbed by the far-left Democrats and the "fake news" media, claiming that they had help from "weak Republicans". The speech ran for a little more than an hour, according to a Wall Street Journal (WSJ) video. I have listed some of the quotes of President

Trump from his January 6th speech that I believe were not only false assertions, but the most inflammatory statements of his speech. These are not in chronological order (all from WSJ).

"They rigged an election like they've never rigged it before."

"We will never give up, we will never concede. It'll never happen, you don't concede when there is theft involved."

"All of us here today do not want to see our election victory stolen by bold and radical left Democrats, which is what they're doing!"

"I've been in two elections, I won 'em both. The second, I won much bigger than the first."

"We will stop the steal."

"It's a pure theft in American History!" "Our election was so corrupt!"

"You will never take back our Country with weakness. You have to show strength, you have to be strong!"

"Today I will lay out some of the evidence that proves that we won this election and we won it by a landslide!"

"After this we're gonna walk downtown, I'll be with you. We're gonna walk down to the

Capitol!"

In all fairness to Mr. Trump, I really don't believe that he understood just how powerful and dangerous his statements were. I also don't believe that Mr. Trump had any knowledge beforehand of the events that transpired during and following his speech on January 6, 2021.

The events to which I am referring happened on Capitol Hill while Congress was in session to validate the 2020 Presidential election via the Electoral College System.

Around 1:00 pm on January 6, 2021, just as Congress started the Electoral vote validation joint session, a group of "Trump-supporters–turned-mob" breached the northwest Capitol security barricades.

Close to 2:00 pm, hundreds of Trump supporters attempted to breach the Capitol eastside barricades, and, for whatever reason, the officers moved the barricades themselves. There were Trump supporters battling overwhelmed and outnumbered Capitol police officers. One officer was hit over the head with a fire extinguisher and sprayed with bear repellant. That officer would later die due to his injuries.

Around 2:15pm the Trump mob actually breached the Capitol doors. I couldn't believe my eyes! Citizens of America were in the Capitol building breaking things (Windows, furniture, etc....), going into Congressional offices, sitting at the desks, stealing things… right outside of the chambers where Congress was convening.

At around 2:30 pm EST, the Capitol police stopped the meeting and informed Vice President Mike Pence and Congress about the mob and the dangerous situation at hand. The Capitol Police then began the evacuation of the chamber, in order to ensure the safety of the Vice President and the Members of Congress. Unfortunately, the officers were only able to evacuate the VP along with about half of the Members of Congress successfully, before the mob reached the chamber, the rest of the members were left, stuck, and scared. The remaining lawmakers in the chamber would endure the torment and anxiety from the uncertainty of their safety until approximately 5:30 pm when the "Sergeant at Arms" finally announced the "all clear!" message.

"Wow!", now, to me, January 6, 2021 was not just a "bad day" in American history, hopefully the horrific events that occurred at our nation's Capital will somehow serve as an "eye opener" for America. I believe that the "attempted" assault on our lawmakers, piloted by deceptive words from a disgruntled politician, although reprehensible, truly has the potential of becoming a much needed "beacon of light" in this tumultuous sea of social unrest from which American is on the verge of drowning.

Jam McNorton

I hope that the events of January 6, 2021, at the Capitol will allow all Americans to see how fragile the psychological fiber of our society is. That day will solidify the importance of each and every American's understanding of the true value of our Democracy, how our leaders have a sworn duty to honor our Democracy, and that our sworn leaders must demonstrate honor for America's Democracy, respecting and adhering to our Democratic process, as well as respecting the tools used to facilitate it.

Chapter 7
America's Law Enforcement: Justice or Just Us?

"I CAN'T BREATHE!"

These were the words of a young Black man by the name of Eric Garner, as the Staten Island police used an illegal chokehold, which eventually cost Eric Garner his life, on July 17, 2014. The police claimed that they were attempting to arrest Garner for selling illegal cigarettes. Black Lives Matter protests broke out all over America in response to the deadly use of force by the police. The officers were not charged.

Sadly, Eric Garner is only one of many un-armed Blacks who have been unjustifiably killed recently because of racist law enforcement officers in America. In Baltimore, Maryland, April 19, 2015, Freddie Gray, 25, died of spinal cord injury a week after being arrested. It is still unclear how he sustained the injury. Officials say he was stopped after fleeing "unprovoked after noticing police presence" and arrested for allegedly possessing a switchblade. He was put in a police van, where they say he suffered a medical emergency.

Stephon Clark, of Sacramento, California, was chased by the Sacramento Police department for allegedly breaking out car windows in South Sacramento at night. While being pursued, Stephon ran into his grandmother's backyard, hoping to evade the police, but the Sacramento Sheriff's helicopter directed the ground police to his location.

Upon reaching Clark's grandmother's house, the two officers walked to the right side of the garage. The side gate was open and the officers saw Stephon with his back to them. The officers demanded to see Clark's hands several times, so Clark finally turned toward the officers with his hands stretched out in front of him to comply with the officers' order. The officers reported that when Clark turned toward them, they thought that he had pointed a gun at them, so they fired 20 shots, hitting Stephon 7 or 8 times. The alleged "gun" turned out to be a cell phone. The shooting occurred on March 18, 2018. On March 2, 2019 the Assistant District Attorney stated that the officers had a right to stop Clark, and that the officers' use of force was justified, no charges filed.

Breonna Taylor, a 26-year-old Black woman, was fatally shot in her Louisville, Kentucky, apartment on March 13, 2020, when White plainclothes officers forced entry into the apartment as part of an investigation into drug dealing operations.

Taylor's boyfriend, Kenneth Walker, was inside with her when the officers knocked on the door and forced entry. Officers said they announced themselves as police before forcing entry, but Walker said he did not hear any announcement, thought the officers were intruders, and fired a warning shot at them. According to officials, it hit one officer in the leg and the officers fired 32 shots in return. Walker was unhurt, but Taylor was hit by six bullets and died. Taylor's home was never searched. (Wikipedia).

I could go on and on about the recent killings of unarmed Blacks by cops, but most of the reports sadly would have the same results; cops murder an unarmed Black person, protests erupt, and charges are rarely filed.

On May 25, 2020, George Floyd, a 46-year-old Black man, was killed by Minneapolis, Minnesota, police. But this one was different. The Black man was unarmed, and, again, thanks to cellular phones and social media, America, along with the entire world, witnessed the boldest exhibition of police brutality, excessive force, and racist murder of an unarmed Black man in history! What made the footage of this "cop killing" of an unarmed Black man gain the attention of the entire world was "how" this unfortunate tragedy was carried out by Minneapolis police office Derek Chauvin.

Apparently on May 25, 2020, George Floyd was being arrested for passing counterfeit money by

Minneapolis police. Chauvin and his team put handcuffs on Mr. Floyd and had him face-down on the pavement in back of the right rear tire of a police cruiser. Officer Derek Chauvin then took his left knee and knelt down on Mr. Floyd's neck. Then Officer Chauvin did something that I had never seen or heard of in my life. There was a bystander videotaping Officer Chauvin kneeling on Floyd's neck, but Chauvin didn't care, as a matter of fact he looked directly into the camera with his right hand in his pocket as if he were posing. This pose lasted for over 8 minutes, showing no emotion, while ignoring George Floyd calling for his mother. Even after Floyd lost consciousness, Officer Chauvin kept kneeling on Floyd's neck until the paramedic asked him to stop.

The video footage sparked a change. It touched the hearts of not just Black people, but also people of all colors, races, creeds, genders, and ages all around the world. A consciousness arose against police brutality that resulted in protests from cities and countries around the globe.

The "change" was the fact that, for once, a city didn't hide the police under their bureaucratic skirt. My hat is off to the Mayor of Minneapolis and the State Attorney General of Minnesota. The officers of this tragic display of how not to protect and serve were fired immediately, and, subsequently, Derek Chauvin was brought up on charges. My condolences to the Floyd family, but please know this folks: George Floyd's inexcusable death served a purpose. His sacrifice is not in vain, God bless you all.

As I've previously stated, racism may not be tangible. It may have no form, but it is definitely one of the most formidable foes we as Americans have ever had to battle. But "together" I believe that, although we may never get rid of it, through humbleness and perseverance we can minimize its effect.

American law enforcement and racial injustice have a long history together. The racial indifferences of Whites vs. Blacks in terms of law enforcement go back as far as slavery and were amplified in the southern states at the end of the Civil War.

This book is not a history lesson, yet at times I find it necessary to search the origin of a problem in order to understand the psychological "climate" of the time in which the behavior of the subject began, in this case, the subject being American law enforcement (local, state, federal) and their protocol policy for policing in America.

If we are seeking to correct a problem of engagement or treatment of people, we must understand the policy, so that we can begin to effectuate change. A complete understanding of the policy will reveal if, in fact, the problem is the policy or you. In the case of American law enforcement, the "rules of engagement" policy for Black people, especially young Black men (no matter what the rule book says) are tainted and need to be corrected. The psychological mindset of the officers can be improved in terms of implicit bias when engaging Blacks, especially young Black men, but before there can be any improvement, these very important, very needed, very appreciated law enforcement officers (without whom we as a society cannot survive, by the way) must be psychologically vetted with non-manipulated lie detectors (and ensuring that "slick" officers are not using drugs or any unnatural additives to beat the vetting). The "vetting" must be done with everyone from the Commissioner and Chief of Police down to the academy cadets (especially the cadets). By honestly vetting our officers, we can accomplish very important goals needed to assess the "psychological climate" of the department. (The only way to correct a problem is to find out who and what the problem is). The things that a human relations test will help to accomplish include, but are not limited to, the following:

1. Identify racist officers;
2. Identify homophobic officers;
3. Identify racially isolated officers;
4. Improve community relations; and
5. Improve the department's ability to police.

There is no easy answer to how to change the police brutality/excessive force situation. I believe that vetting and reforming the ways in which our much-needed police officers engage Black people or any civilian will help. We have a lot of good police, but, unfortunately, we also have a lot of racist officers.

Racial Profiling: The "Jim Crow" Policing

After the Civil War between the northern and southern states ended, and Black slaves became "free men," many of the southern states' ex-slave owners did not want slaves to be freed. To get around this, states like South Carolina and Mississippi created and enacted the "Black Code Laws." These laws basically said that freed slaves had to show the ability to demonstrate financial stability, or they had to work for the landowners for free. If the slaves could not or would not do either, they could be jailed and beaten publicly. Basically, it would be volunteer slavery.

Around 1910, until 1964, "Jim Crow" laws were instituted for Blacks. "Separate but equal" is how the Supreme Court named the legal demoralizing treatment of Blacks. Separate restrooms, dining, water fountains. If a Black person was seated on public transportation (bus, train, etc.), and a White person wanted the seat, the Black person would have to give up the seat, no matter how old they were. In 1955, in Montgomery, Alabama, Rosa Parks, a Black woman, refused to give up her seat to a White man. This started the Civil Rights movement, and, through the efforts of people like Ms. Parks, the folks conducting the Greensboro sit-in, Dr. Martin Luther King, and Black civil rights activists, the Civil Rights

Act of 1964 was passed.

What do Civil Rights have to do with law enforcement today? The truth is that the manner in which law enforcement officers treat Black people, especially Black men, has a lot to do with Civil Rights, "Jim Crow" laws, and the Black Code laws. This is demonstrated in what is known as "Racial Profiling."

Black Code laws and "Jim Crow" laws meant that there were two justice systems in America, but supposedly the Civil Rights Act of 1964 would put an end to the two justice systems. The two justice systems, one for Whites and one for Blacks and other minorities, but especially Black people, was unfair back then, and today it is still unfair. Examples of the double standard were shown in the 1994 Crime Bill.

The 1994 Crime Bill was enacted by Congress as a tool to fight the "war on drugs." The 1994 Crime Bill, better known as the "crack law" was one of the most unfair, biased laws in modern history. The "crack law" imposed a federal mandatory minimum sentence of 5 years for trafficking 500 grams of powder cocaine. The reason the law was so racially biased is because the lawmakers made a 100 to 1 double standard for crack versus powder cocaine. This meant that a crack dealer (90% of whom were Black) would receive a 5-year mandatory sentence for 5 grams of crack, which was simply cocaine purified by cooking it in baking soda and water. This allowed the cocaine to be smoked. Critics tried to justify the 100 to 1 crack versus powder cocaine sentencing by stating that crack smoking made people violent. That was a lie. The real truth was that Blacks controlled 90% of the crack market, while Whites and Hispanics controlled the powder market. The "crack law" was a way to lock up Blacks.

The point is that from the federal government to the street cops, Blacks are engaged, policed, and sentenced much more harshly than Whites. There have been a lot of Blacks who have been killed by law enforcement for anything from "traffic stops" to minor violations such as "selling cigarettes." A lot of this comes from the psychological mindset of racial profiling by the officers. Consequently, a minor stop ends up turning into an unjustified "police involved" shooting.

Jam McNorton

Chapter 8
Racist Whites: The "New" Slaves

"If it ain't white, it ain't right!"

It's got to be hard to have to live around people who you hate. You wish that the world was filled with people who you like and love, but worlds like that usually only exist in dreams. The reality is that the world we live in, especially America, is filled with people of virtually every color, race, gender, age, and, now, transgender.

Bummer, huh? I mean, why the Hell do I have to share my country with Niggers? I don't understand why they can't just go back to their own country! America belongs to White people, don't it? These might be your racist complaints and beliefs, but the truth is that America belongs to Americans, not just White people. As far as the question why Black people can't just go back to their own country, the fact is that, if the Blacks that you are inquiring about are Americans, then they are in their own country; it's called America.

How long do racist Whites plan to keep suffering without a cause? Please allow me to explain.

Jam McNorton

When the relationship between racist White people and Black people began, White people were slave owners, and Black people were slaves. This was a long time ago, and times have changed. As a matter of fact, there are no slave owners alive today. The only "slave owner" still alive is racism itself, and the only slaves that are still alive en-masse are racist White people, themselves.

Think about it instead of trying to hide behind getting mad because I called racist White people slaves. If in fact you are suffering from being a White racist, then I feel sorry for you, and you are the reason I wrote this book to hopefully help you to understand that you don't have to continue to hate Black people. You don't have to keep feeling uptight whenever you encounter, have to engage with, or are around Black people. You don't have to continue believing something and really not know why.

October 1979. I was 16 years old in high school in my hometown of Santa Maria, California. On this particular day, the State of California was offering an aptitude test to the group of academic students of which I was a part. The group was called the "MGM" or Mentally Gifted Minors.

On this day, we were the group of students who had been chosen for the California Academic Challenge. The prize was early graduation for anyone who passed the test!

Great! But, to catch up with my story, we have to go back to the 6:00 PM local news the night before the test. That night, there was an announcement on the local news that the local chapter of the Ku Klux Klan was going to be holding a rally at Lopez Lake at 12 noon the next day, and the newscaster advised that anyone who wasn't part of the group should avoid going to Lopez Lake tomorrow. Well, that was the day of the test.

I get to the classroom at about 5 minutes to eight, and, of course, the test started at 8:00 AM. "Thank you, Jesus, I made it!" All right, I run in the classroom and up to the instructor's desk. He frowns at me over his Coke-bottle glasses, as he points to the clock. After his ten-second rebuke, he hands me a test, a number 2 pencil, and scratch paper, and I take a seat next to a redheaded kid. After the instructor's speech about "no calculators, blah, blah, blah," he says, "You may begin."

We had four hours to complete the test, and that was cool. Everything was going smoothly. All of the sudden, at around 10 minutes after 11:00, I notice that my neighbor, the redheaded kid, starts panicking, looking at the clock and rushing through the test, and he is only halfway done. About 10 minutes later I finish, and I look over, and the kid is going through a minor anxiety attack. So, I ask him what is wrong? He shakes his head and says, "I gotta go. I can't be late."

Jam McNorton

I remembered the news from the night before and the "Klan" rally. I say, "Why are you rushing? Where do you have to be that is so important?" He just turns his head to the right without answering, so I said while laughing, "Where you going, Lopez Lake?" He turns his head left and looks me in my eyes with the most painful look I had ever seen. I stop laughing and say, "You don't want to go do you?" He just put his eyes toward the ground and didn't reply. I put my hand on his shoulder and say, "Hey man, you ain't gotta go. Tell 'em you had to take a test to graduate early." The kid picks up his unfinished test and materials and, as he heads up to the instructor's desk, he turns toward me and says, "I gotta."

I felt so bad for that kid. Oh yeah, I passed the test and graduated at 16.

I know in my heart that this young man isn't the only person who has been "forced" into being a racist White person. I believe in the human ability to "see" the truth, the ability to have a change of heart, despite one's prior beliefs or upbringing. I believe in our human ability to "see through" lies and unfounded teachings. I believe that every human has the innate ability to change, to love, to forgive, and to coexist in peace.

I don't believe that there is one racist White person who lives or works around Black people on a constant basis, who doesn't have at least one Black person who they love, whether this is an old Black man or woman, somebody who they go to school with, or a child, but there is someone in their circle who they don't hate, who they like and, actually, really love. Now they might justify their caring for this person by saying that this person is different or "He ain't like the other Niggers." But however, it is justified, I believe that if their lives are entwined, all racist White people have one or more Black people they care about.

My book is to let you know that you don't have to keep hating Black people. You are stronger than the lies; you are stronger than the peer pressure. I am praying that God will release all racist White people and free them, once and for all, from the slave owner named "Racism!"

I care about and love all racist White people, because I believe that, in time, you will be freed from racism. Please understand that Black people love you, and that the truth is that all the misguided hate you have is unnecessary.

Hate: the real "slave driver"

Have you ever considered how much energy it takes to hate a person or a group of people? Well, how about the amount of energy and effort it takes to hate someone just because of their race or the color of their skin? In my experience it takes more energy to hate than to love. Now for the big question: Consider a person with whom you interact a lot. Let's say that you work with them, and you have worked with this person for a long time, years. You and this person have never argued and, aside from being an excellent workmate, the truth is that this person possesses all of the attributes that you personally desire in someone:

Hardworking Honest
Kind Loyal Respectful
A good sense of humor Caring
Attractive
Always has your back Great to be around
Minds their own business
They trust your judgment

Now what if this person is Black and what if you are a racist White person who has grown up hating Black people all of your life. Can you honestly tell yourself or anyone else that you hate this person who exemplifies all of the qualities that you look for in people? Can you honestly say that you hate being around this person? If the answer to either question is "yes," you are lying to yourself. If this person were White, wouldn't they be in your inner circle? You don't hate this person; you love being around this person. It's what's on the inside that matters in life. How would you feel in the same situation if you were actually blind? See, that wasn't hard, huh?

There is a reason that this author is concerned with telling racist White people that they don't have to be a slave to an emotion, a non-tangible slave owner called "Racism." You don't have to be uptight when you encounter Black people because you are being driven by unjustified hatred.

Chapter 9
The "Ball & Chain Syndrome"

"Half of my family would greet you with open arms, but the other half would have a rope waitin'!"

February 1981. I had just started "Tech" school at Chanute Air Force Base, Illinois. A couple of airmen and I decided to go hang out with the college kids at the University of Illinois. It was a Friday night, and we decided to hit the college bars right outside of the school in Champagne-Urbana. It was snowing and cold, but we didn't care. Once we got in the bar and had a few beers we didn't even think about the weather. "Man!! Look at all the girls!" one of the guys said. I remember telling the other guy with us to "close his mouth," 'cause he was literally drooling. We were really having a good time.

A little after 1 AM, I was sitting in the booth by myself, just watching all the people dancing, when a beautiful White girl with a beautiful shape, olive complexion, and blonde hair down to her butt walked up and asked if she could sit down. I was drunk, Black, and 17 years old. I rubbed my eyes to make sure I wasn't dreaming, and, to my surprise, she was still there when the rubbing stopped! "Damn! Damn! Damn!" I thought.

My mama taught me good manners, so I stood up, and she sat down, then I joined her and introduced myself. I told her my name was Keith, and that I was here for Tech school at Chanute A.F.B. She said that her name was Lisa and that she was finishing up her last year at the University. Then she said something that blew me away. She asked me if I wanted to go to her place. I immediately said, "Yes!" so, we went back to her apartment. She lived close to the school, so we walked.

Her place was nice; it was only about 4 or 5 blocks from the bar, but it could've been in Arizona, because I didn't know where I was anyway.

I ended up spending the weekend with Lisa, and she drove me back to the base Sunday night. I was in love, or so I thought I was. Looking back after all of these years, I realize that it really was the fact that I was green and with a beautiful girl, an older White girl who wanted to be with me despite the color of my skin, more likely because of the color of my skin.

I wound up spending every weekend with Lisa, and it was great! So, the last weekend before I was to graduate from Tech school and fly out to my permanent base, which was going to be Nellis Air Force Base, Nevada (Las Vegas), we were laying on the couch watching a movie. Lisa had been acting weird, real quiet, so I finally said, "What's wrong?" Lisa was sitting to the right of me and when I asked her what was wrong, she turned to me, fell into my chest, and started crying inconsolably. She was crying so hard that I almost started crying. "Hey beautiful, talk to me, what's wrong? Did I do something wrong?"

"No! Well… yes, yes you did something," she said. "I have been at school for three and a half years. Guys always tried to pursue me, but I never liked any of them! Then, out of nowhere, here you appeared, and in seven weeks, you made me fall in love with you, and now you're leaving?!! For real?!! I don't want you to go, but I know you must. So, what do I do now?"

"Hey…I don't want to go either, and I'm in love with you, too. You're not the only one hurting! I'm hurting, too, baby. I know what we can do after you graduate in June. You can move to Las Vegas, and we can get married, if you want to! Do you want to marry me?"

Lisa looked at me with her big pretty blue eyes, and she said, "Are you serious? Don't play with me, Keith; yes, I want to marry you. I'm extra rich, so money's not a problem. The only problem that I can think of is my family."

"Your family? What's the problem with your family?" I said.

She turned away, crying. Then she turned back to me and said, "Okay, well you're gonna find out anyway, so it might as well be now. It's like this: I have a big family, and the problem is that half of my family would greet you with open arms… but the other half would have a rope waiting."

I didn't know what to say. Nonetheless, I lied and committed to marriage anyway, but after I got to Nellis, I never heard from Lisa again.

Stories like this are common, sadly. The title of this chapter is "The Ball & Chain Syndrome," and, yes, the title is metaphorically speaking of a "marriage." The marriage in this case is referring to the problems of being connected to a racist group (family or friends), while not being a racist, yourself.

Do you know how many half Black, half White kids unfairly only know half of their family members? This is because the kids are not accepted by the White racist side of their family. These situations of "forced alienation" of these children is exceptionally hard on the kids' self-esteem.

Years ago, in the South, if a Black man was caught with a White woman, the Black man would be hanged. Surprisingly, even today in 2022, it's not easy for Black men to be with White women, especially in the South.

A lot of White racists claim that the reason that they detest mixing with any other race is because they want to keep the White race pure. But the real reason is foolish pride. White racist men don't want Black men to impregnate the White women, but the racist White men, throughout history, have impregnated Black women more than Black men have impregnated White women, another double standard.

Past the intimate relationship view, children of racist Whites are rarely allowed to befriend Black children, further deepening the racial divide.

Please understand the importance of allowing yourself a chance to live life without worrying about what your friends or family will think about your choice not to be a racist. The healing has to begin with you, and, more importantly, the beliefs that you pass on to your children. In other words—if you really don't hate Black people, is it right to teach your kids to hate because of "family traditions"?

It is a shame to see some of the young White people struggling with their identity, especially the students in high school and college. A lot of the youngsters starting high school, or even college who were, unfortunately, raised in a racist family, get caught in between how they were taught and what they actually experience, as far as their perception of Blacks. See, being told "how" people are and actually experiencing "how" people often turns out to be as different as "night and day."

The problems start to build up inside the hearts and minds of these very impressionable, curious children of racist White people, most of whom have been isolated from interacting with Black folk on a regular basis until now.

It's important to take a moment to take a look at the beauty of the human mind.

Out of all the living organisms on earth, the human being has the most advanced mind of all. The human mind has a special entity within its makeup that is so demanding that it virtually will not rest until it is satisfied. Neuroscientists might call this entity the Frontal Lobe, but I'll simply call it the logic section of the brain.

This is my theory: the logical part of the human mind is the reason we won't let a record player keep "skipping." This part of the brain talks to your motor skills department, and, together, they allow the arm and needle to be lifted off of the "skipping" record. Your logical section is the reason the mechanic at the auto repair shop keeps trying different things until the car's problem is fixed.

This demanding "troubleshooter" is the reason young children of racist White people are struggling with their "identity." The logical section is in conflict with what the kids were taught about Black people, versus how they are experiencing Black people, now that these young students get to interact with Black students.

The conflict is whether or not to continue being racist, especially in college. The reason I believe that the racist White students' identity (belief system) is in conflict with itself, is because the young people are maturing, and the "logic" portion of their mind will not be satisfied with what the mind has been told to "experience" after it proves to be contrary to the teachings. Friendships are forged, and myths about Blacks are erased, and the walls of hate are torn down, with bridges built in their place. Now, this isn't true with all racist students. Some racist White students hang with other racist White students, forming "hate clubs" and such, and, thus, their identity (belief system) of being racist stays intact, regardless of their Black experience.

In conclusion, the "Ball & Chain Syndrome" that children of White racist people have to deal with has to be hard on them, especially the racist children that change their beliefs and choose not to hate Black people anymore. The saddest situations that I have seen are when the children of racist White families develop intimate personal relationships, get married, and have kids with Blacks and end up being ousted from the family.

Chapter 10
Intra-Racism: Based on Nationality

The last time that I spoke nostalgically in the book to you good people, I was in the Air Force. To fill in the empty spots since our last talk, I left the Air Force in 1989, after serving eight years on active duty. Upon my discharge, I left my final duty station which was at McClellan AFB in Sacramento, CA. I moved back to my home town of Santa Maria, CA. Santa Maria was, and still is, a relatively small agricultural town located on the central coast of California, between Santa Barbara and San Luis Obispo. I moved to San Diego in 1990, with two of my childhood friends.

August, 1990 – San Diego, CA, was really beautiful, and we lived less than a mile from the beach in a suburb called Imperial Beach. I had only been there a month, when I decided to stay. In order to stay, I realized that I should probably find a job. I mean, it made sense. I wasn't exactly rolling in the dough.

I bought a Ford Pinto and an acoustic guitar, and, until I landed a job, I would drive down to the beach and play my guitar on a little wooden

Jam McNorton

bench along the boardwalk, as I watched the majestic waves roll in and out. One day, I noticed a very beautiful brown-skinned young lady sitting not far from where I was playing. She looked to be in her early twenties and she was gorgeous! She wore a short Jheri-curl, had hazel eyes and modest makeup, and, although it was still summer, she dressed conservatively, a nice short set, and her shoes were simple sandals.

She was there, day after day, always painting with an easel, and, on her breaks, she read a book of poetry.

On one particular day, her presence pricked my heart. She was seated catty-corner to my right. I was just doing my thing like always, playing my guitar, when, all of the sudden, I felt heat on the right side of my head, as if someone was starring. I turned to the right to investigate my feelings, and, when I did, I was staring right where she happened to be sitting. Now, what's crazy is that every time I would turn, I would catch a glimpse of her staring, then she would lower her eyes back to her book! I didn't want her to think I was a creep, so I would turn back to the ocean. This cycle continued for a while, and then I slipped into a musical trance. A musical trance is when a musician or singer experiences a bonding with their craft. This moment of memorable musical excellence is usually realized during a performance when improvisation is inserted.

I was having a musical moment, playing while freestyling lyrics, when something told me to turn toward the beautiful girl, so I did, only this time, she didn't have her book in her hands for her eyes to run to. Instead, she had a paint brush in her right hand and when I looked, she was staring, mouth open, as if star struck! When she realized that our eyes had finally met, because she didn't have her book, her duck and cover impulse made her turn to the easel. However she did it so fast, she didn't realize that her right arm was already extended with the paint brush in hand so when she turned towards the canvas she painted a stripe across her entire painting!

It was a gut-busting moment, and that is when we finally met for the first time. I stopped singing and playing, and she just froze. It was pure unadulterated comedy. She sat in front of her painting, not saying a word, with the culprit paintbrush in her hand. She was in suspended animation.

"Ahhhh, ha, ha, haaa," I laughed, then, while I was laughing at her, I fell backwards off the bench into the sand. I'm lying in the sand, guitar on my chest, and I couldn't stop laughing. I had tears coming out of my eyes. All of the sudden, I felt a slap on my right shoulder. Not a hard slap, it was more like a playful "you're making fun of me" slap.

I heard a voice say with a beautiful foreign accent, "Don't laugh at me!"

Jam McNorton

The voice was close, so close it made me stop laughing for a minute. I turned to the right and could swear I was dreaming. I'm lying on my back, in the sand, my guitar on my chest, tears of laughter running down my face, and sitting in the sand on her legs with her beautiful, innocent self, right next to me, was the "Artist".

"Hi", I said.

"I thought you were nice, but then you laughed at me! That is mean. Maybe my thoughts of you were wrong. Maybe you are not nice," she replied.

So, I sat up with my guitar now on my lap. I pulled the strap over my head and laid my guitar on my left side in the sand and said "I apologize".

"Hey, how about we start over? My name is Keith, Keith McNorton, and I think you are beautiful! What's your name?"

"I don't think I should tell you," she said.

"Aw, come on, I already apologized, and I told you my name. Please?" "If you really mean it, Mean Man!"

"I do, I really do," I said emphatically.

"Okay, I am Neeva, Neeva Udu".

So, then I said "Neeva? Neeva Udu?"

"Yes", she said, "Why? Are you going to laugh at my name now Mean Man?"

"No, not at all, I love your name. You're from Africa?" I asked.

"Yes."

"What part of Africa?" "Ghana", she responded.

"Okay", I said. "Well, I'm from a small town called Santa Maria, it's about 300 miles north of here".

"I really like your music!" she said enthusiastically.

"I really like your art! Especially the one you are working on now!"

The realization of the accidental paint brush stripe hit out minds at the same time and we both started laughing. We laughed so hard that tears of laughter were flowing down both our faces. She kept slapping my shoulder and saying "Don't laugh! Don't laugh!" And then it happened.

We had developed a cycle, she would say "Don't laugh!" and I would say "okay, okay". We would have silence for about five seconds before we would start busting up again. This cycle stopped when she was laughing so hard she fell on my chest. It felt so right that neither one of us moved.

We laid in the sand for what seemed like forever. We fell asleep, and when we awoke, we shared one of the most awesome sunsets I could have ever imagined.

"Who... are... you?" she asked quizzically

"Who... are... you?" I inquired.

Then, she kissed my cheek and returned her head to my chest. I returned the gesture by gently lifting her chin with my right index finger. As our souls were finally introduced eye to eye. We drove to each other's heart through a slow, sumptuous kiss, the kind of kiss that you hope will never end.

After that day, we were inseparable. We were always together for fun in the sun, picnics on the beach, feeding bread to the seagulls, racing in the sand, rolling over and over in the low tide, pure bliss!

I finally landed a job with a Naval Contractor, installing fiber optic systems on the navy ships out at Point Loma Naval Station. New job, new girl--a beautiful African Princess named NEEVA UDU!!! To me, life was sweet... or so I thought.

For the next two months, I felt like I was riding in a giant hot air balloon. Then, one Saturday morning, I was awakened by someone tapping on my bedroom window. "Hold on. Who is it?" I asked.

"It's me!" I heard and right away I knew it was my sweet baby. Her voice sounded really distressed. It sounded like it was mixed with tears.

"Wait Neeva, here I come, love!" I got up and ran to the front door in my underwear. I was staying with my Homeboy Michael, as were other folks. I didn't care who was there. Getting to the front door was the only mission on my mind at that time. Protocol would have to wait!

I opened the door, and who I saw was Neeva, but what I saw was a lost little fawn who looked like she had gotten separated from her mother, scared and very confused.

"What's wrong Baby?!" I asked. She held her head down, put her arms around my waist and leaned into my chest crying. "Come on baby, you got me standing half- naked in the doorway, let's go to my room." She wouldn't move, and she wouldn't let me move. I could feel the tears running down my chest. "Neeva, please baby, it's gonna be alright, whatever it is, okay? Let's go to my room," I pleaded.

At the time, what I'd said about "everything

going to be alright" sounded good, but man, was I in for a surprise.

We moved to my room, and I put on some smooth jazz to try and help Neeva relax. After I put on the music, I put on jeans and a shirt and then sat down on the bed with my back up against the headboard. Neeva was lying on the bed, her arms tucked under the pillow with her head turned toward the window, just staring at the wall underneath.

Finally, after an hour of silence and my anxiety level making my left eye twitch, I couldn't take it anymore. "What's wrong babe? Is it something I said or did? Cuz if I did something, I know I didn't mean to, but I don't know what I could have possibly done as you are the best thing that has ever happened to me, and I love you, and I'm going crazy right now," I rambled on. Moments passed before Neeva turned toward me and laid her head on my hip up against my stomach. So, I put my arm across her ribs and I gently rubbed her stomach. That always seemed to calm her.

"I can't see you anymore," she said.

I believe that was the hardest swallow in history. Then my heart started racing, barely able to speak, I said something like "Wha, wha, what!?"

"I cannot see you anymore," she repeated.

"Did you find someone else? Do you have to

move? Cause, you can live with me if you want to," I said with hope.

Then my little beautiful artist sat up on the edge of the bed next to me and in the midst of my rambling, she put her index finger on my lips to stop my ranting.

"It's not for any of the reasons that you question," she murmured.

"Then why? Please tell me."

"It's complicated," she said.

"Try me," I retorted.

"My family will not allow me to see you. If we continue with our relationship, my family will disown me," she whimpered.

"Disown you? Why? Do they want us to get married?" I inquired.

"No, as I said, it's complicated. I have a very traditional family, and, although I do not agree with some of their rules, I must obey".

"Rules? What rules does your family have that would not allow you to be with me?" I said at a loss.

"We are not permitted to date or marry outside of our own, unless it is absolutely necessary," she responded.

"Outside of your OWN? I don't understand, I'm Black, and you're Black, so what's the problem?" I asked.

"It's not easy for me to explain, because no matter how I try, I cannot stop the truth from hurting you," she cried.

"What do you mean? I thought you liked being with me?" I said.

"Like? NO Keith, I LOVE being with you! You are wonderful, kind, and caring, and I'm sure that I'm falling in love with you. The problem is that although we are both Black, my people do not recognize American Blacks as African. Therefore, our relationship will not be respected by my people, and I know that you don't understand, but that is how it is. I am very sorry," she said.

With that said, Neeva stood up with tears flowing. She leaned over to where I was sitting and kissed me. Then she walked to my bedroom door, turned with red-crying eyes, and said, "Goodbye."

This chapter is different from the previous chapters because it doesn't have citations. It's based purely on my opinion of the problem between American Blacks and Africans.

"Although we are both Black, my people do not recognize American Blacks as African."

When the young lady, Neeva, made that statement to me back in 1990, I didn't give it much credibility. At the time, I truly believed that she was merely using her people's dislike for Black Americans as an excuse to stop seeing me.

I am very sad to admit that, 30 years later, in 2022, not only have I changed my perception of what Neeva meant when she said that, but I have also, over the years, come to understand and believe that what she said it true.

<u>The African Wall</u>

A lot of people have been conditioned to believe that, for someone to commit an act of racism toward someone else, the perpetrator would have to belong to a different race from the victim. But what if you are receiving the same biased, mistreatment from people of your own race?

Specifically, straight up, straight out, I am speaking about the pain and anguish, the feeling of not being worthy, not being good enough for the approval of the Motherland. We are little baby birds, a whole nation of us. Our mouths have been open for years waiting to be nourished by our African brothers and sisters, yet, no matter how hard we hope, no matter how much we try, and no matter how much we are willing, all of our efforts shatter at the African Wall of Alienation, blame, and excuses. We are Black Americans needing our Africans!

If we can experience just part of the love our African brothers and sisters have so honorably expressed for our loved one George Floyd (rest in heavenly peace, my brother) the Wall will fall, and the healing can begin.

My African brothers and sisters, it doesn't matter what you think Black Americans think of you, the Devil is a lie. We don't think anything bad about any of you. How can we? We don't know you.

In order to break down the wall between Black Americans and Africans, let me, a Black American, clear the air:

1. We don't think Africans are scammers or anything bad. We don't judge anyone.

2. Black Americans are regular people--we have people that scam, kill, sell drugs, do all manner of things, just like every other race. We also, just like any other race, have caring, loving, law abiding, hard-working people. Black Americans want to know our African family.

3. Instead of stating that we are wild beasts (Akata) or that we are lazy, why can't my African brothers and sisters take the time to teach Black Americans work ethic or the value

of seizing opportunities afforded to Black Americans in America, instead of using your judgement of us as an excuse to keep us out of your lives?

I hope that my African brothers and sisters who have blessed me by reading my book, take notice that I say "Black Americans" and never use "African Americans" to describe myself or my American-born Black brothers and sisters. There are a couple of reasons why.

1. Until Black Americans and Africans succeed at tearing down the African Wall that separates Blacks from Africans, and we, as Black Americans, are truly accepted as "Africans" by African people, I choose my ethnicity to be described as "Black American."

2. Once we, as Blacks, truly believe that we are recognized, accepted, and respected by the African Union, it is only then that we should be called American Africans, not, "African Americans."

Finally, I need my African brothers and sisters to hear what I am about to say:

The Greatest Pain

The pain of being rejected by our African brothers and sisters hurts Black Americans more than the 400 years of oppression we have suffered at the hands of racist White people.

Jam McNorton

To have to continue being alienated from the people of the land that we, as Black people, have been told all our lives is our heritage and, in many cases, have been told to go home to by racist Whites, is unbearable and just not right. Especially when we are denied access to our people and heritage because of false narratives expressed by the very people we need and want to know and love.

"OUR AFRICAN BROTHERS AND SISTERS, THIS HAS TO CHANGE!"

Love, Black America!!!

Hate Without a Cause

Chapter 11
The Mirror

All of my life, people have tried to give me advice, especially if I was doing something wrong. The problem was (besides what I did wrong) that no matter how they tried, I wouldn't concede. They could show me all the proof that I was wrong— it didn't matter. "I" was in charge of me, and the situation, or so I thought. So, in order to stop their "preaching," I would argue with them, justify, dignify, clarify and some more "-FYS," anything to get them off my back. I would lie to them and even try to lie to myself. Lying to people was easy, but lying to myself never worked. I could tell myself the lie, but it wasn't the lie that kept me doing the wrong. I understand now that it was my addiction that drove me.

Addiction comes in many forms. For me, it was my addiction to drugs. The reason I am speaking about addiction is important in reference to racial hate. Addiction plays a role in a person's choices. Now, the type of addiction I am speaking of is not drugs or alcohol. The type of addiction that I am speaking of, as far as fueling White racist people's hate for Blacks, is the addiction to "peer approval." I went to school with White racists. I worked with and for White racist people, and most are easier to deal with when they are by themselves. Get them around their racist family or friends, especially if drinking alcohol is part of the encounter, and oh boy! Black jokes, the "N-word," yeah all of that.

Why am I speaking about racist Whites being addicted to "peer approval"? It's because I believe that a lot of those who claim to be a "White is right" racist who hates Black people are really not as "racist" as they claim to be, and really, that's a good thing. I have an exercise called "The Mirror" that will help people prove to themselves if their choice to hate Black people is valid or not. (This exercise, of course, can only help if its questions are answered honestly.)

When I previously mentioned how people would try to give advice to convince me about my wrongdoings, I explained that I could lie to people, but I couldn't lie to myself. This is why the exercise is called "The Mirror." The exercise, if honestly completed, will give anyone who completes it a chance to do a little "introspection," or, in other words, "a chance to look within yourself." Hopefully, by taking this voyage, 1 of 2 facts will be revealed:

1. A person's reasons for hating Black people are valid.
2. A person's reasons for hating Black people are not valid.

If, after honestly completing this exercise, a person who harbors racist impulses toward Black people find that fact #2 is true for themselves, they may find that they do not have to keep hating Blacks, for the fact that they have no valid reason.

Whether or not they actually choose to stop hating Black people, at least they will know the truth about their excuses for hating Black people. If you can't give concrete answers, please just answer "I don't know" or "Nothing," not "I don't know,

I just hate Blacks," or "They are different," or "They stink," etc.

This is for you.

White Racist Validity Test: Black Hate

The following test questions are not to determine if you are a racist. The test questions in this specific type of exercise will be used to determine two points:

1. Do you hate Black people?

2. Are your reasons for hating Blacks valid?

[The answers for the following test questions are for your eyes only, unless you choose to disclose them.]

1. Do you have a problem accepting Blacks as equal to Whites?

If yes, why?

2. Do you have a problem with more than one Black family living in your neighborhood?

If yes, why?

3. Do you communicate with Blacks in the same manner as Whites?

If no, why not?

4. Do you hate or dislike Blacks?

If yes, why?

5. What have Blacks done to Whites or to you for you to hate them?

6. Do you hate Blacks by your own choice, or because your friends or family hate them?

7. Do you have proof to corroborate your reasons for hating Blacks?

If yes, what proof?

8. Do you live in a neighborhood or town where hating Blacks is demanded of you?

9. Why is expressing hate for Blacks so important?

10. Did you decide to hate Blacks on your own, or were you persuaded by someone?

Jam McNorton

This completes the test. I hope that the questions were a benefit for you, and that this exercise provides a chance to learn a little more about yourself.

My goal for this test is to help a person who may be suffering as a racist person (or so they may think) will have a chance to break free from the bondage of unjustified hate toward Black people. Especially if the choice is to hate Blacks is due to peer pressure from family, friends, or the town they live in. In other words, I pray that this test can be a sort of magnifying glass for you of your true feelings and beliefs. I hope that this test showed racist Whites or anyone that they do not have to hate Blacks anymore.

Chapter 12
The "New Generation"

"There is only once race, the "Human Race," and the rainbow is necessary!"
- Jam McNorton

Did you notice that this chapter is called "The 'New Generation'"? Most people would assume that there might be a "typo," or a mistake in the name, like maybe I was meaning to name this chapter: "The Next Generation." Well, just to be clear, I named the chapter exactly for the purpose intended.

The "New Generation" has nothing to do with age. As a matter of fact, to me this generation that I am speaking of is comprised of people of all ages, colors, races, creeds, genders, and transgenders. We saw the birth of this group of people in America, as well as around the world, come to life after the May 25, 2020, killing of George Floyd by Minneapolis, Minnesota, police. It was like a beautiful, long-needed dream, people all around the world protesting American police brutality.

Amazingly, there is one person who caused the worldwide protest of all races, and that person ironically is Officer Derek Chauvin of the

Jam McNorton

Minneapolis Police Department.

Black Lives Matter protests against police brutality have been going on for a while. The thing is, most of the protests were mostly comprised of Blacks and Hispanics, and a few White people (thank you to everyone). But when Officer Derek Chauvin displayed his inexcusable arrogance by kneeling on Mr. Floyd's neck with his right hand in his pocket, looking directly into the camera as if he was posing, for over eight minutes, he touched the hearts of people all over the world and put a spotlight on racial hate.

This is 2022, and times and people are changing. I live in Sacramento, California, a city of many faces. Besides being the capital of California, Sacramento has a few diverse "race relation" climates. I live in South Sacramento, in the neighborhood of Oak Park, a racially balanced, impoverished part of Sacramento.

There are a lot of homeless in Sacramento of all races, due to many reasons, and with this COVID-19 virus pandemic, the city of Sacramento is currently battling not only homelessness, we are battling "sick" homelessness as well, like most cities in America in 2022. Amazingly, there have not been any racial problems in the homeless camps, as though there is a "code of respect" amongst the coexisting races trying to survive. Thank God for civility in the homeless camps, but that is only one of the city's racial climates. Another racial climate in Sacramento is the "Pro-Trumpers," a right-wing conservative group that mainly live in the surrounding cities in Sacramento County. The trip is that since the George Floyd situation in May of 2020, the conservative right wing groups have not been as vocal (racially speaking) and, to this author, this is definitely a sign of change, a much welcomed one.

I am encouraged by the consciousness of Americans (and the world, for that matter) on the subject of racism and the unfairness of policing for Blacks. To me, this is a start, a real chance to begin the task of tearing down racial "walls" and replacing these divides with meaningful racial bridges.

Someone once told me that there will always be racist bigots in America, so we are really wasting our time with this "Black Lives Matter crap." What is so crazy is that the person was Black!

My reply to him is the same thing I want everyone to hear, "All" lives matter, but all lives are not getting unfairly slain by our police.

If it were Whites getting killed by the police, we would be saying White Lives Matter or whatever race of people, but until every race matters, none of them do!

With this "New Generation" of people of all races, ages, colors, creeds, genders, and transgenders marching in solidarity with Black folk, I am convinced that, although we may never totally abolish racism, together we can limit the public systemic effects of racism. With the backing of new laws and each race of people really learning to respect the inalienable rights of life, liberty, and the pursuit of happiness guaranteed to "all" Americans, we can get rid of the belief of "superior and inferior" statuses for one race above the others. No, I don't believe in socialism or communism, I believe in "fair" capitalism, by a fair democratic government for a fair democratic society.

I believe that most people of all walks of life are tired of the hatred that racist White people exude toward Blacks. I believe that we as Americans are at a very important "crossroads" in race relations and human equity. What do I mean when I speak on human equity? I mean the "New Generation" is not only concerned about police brutality and the police killing of unarmed Blacks, but they are also fighting for equity for Americans of all races, creeds, colors, genders, and transgenders.

For the first time in my life, I am truly excited about my hope that America is really finally ready to do more about the White racist hate for Black people than just talk about it. People have known about the problem for centuries, and although I must admit that some progress has been made over the years, I feel as though we as a nation are at a very "pivotal" point. The reason my hope is getting stronger is due to the increase of White people in America protesting against police brutality towards unarmed Blacks.

Conclusion

> Open your eyes and see,
> if we're gonna make things better,
> we're gonna have to make a change...
> face the reality,
> the world was made for you and me...
>
> - Jam McNorton

"HATE WITHOUT A CAUSE," wow... I hope that you enjoyed the book. Now it's time to sum it all up, so I will do my best!

I started the book identifying racism, a terrible monster that has no form, and we found out that racism is a belief that one race of people is superior to all other races.

Our next stop on our journey took us to "White Superiority"—the Lie, where we learned that White people are not superior to any other race, but because the White racist founding fathers feared reprisals from newly freed Black slaves, the founding fathers under America's reconstruction era told White Americans that White people would be categorized as superior, and Blacks would be categorized as inferior, in order for the two races to coexist in America.

The question of why White racist people hate Blacks still remained. There is no viable reason, even after mistreatment comparison charts of

Whites and Blacks proved that from slavery to present day, Black people have not done anything to the White race as a whole to merit being hated.

So here is my final summation of the book: White people, Blacks and all other races according to our Declaration of Independence have been created equal. God gave all of us "freedom of choice," and that is truly a right that cannot be denied. So, in truth, we all have the right to choose who we like, who we love, who we dislike, and even who we hate. What we, as Americans, don't have the right to do is to allow our choices to deny, personally or systemically, any other American their rights to life, liberty, and the pursuit of happiness that are guaranteed to all Americans.

Finally, America, we have made a lot of progress as a nation - economically, technologically, in medicine—and truly we have improved the rights of Blacks and all races under the law.

Where we continue to suffer is in our inability as a nation to deal with the race relation problems between racist Whites and the Black race as a whole. It is time for the truth to come forward. Why? Because this unfounded "hate" that racist Whites keep pushing toward Blacks is costing Black lives, hurting Black businesses, and equally hurting White people who are afraid to show love to Blacks, because they are related to these racist Whites. My objective for writing this book is not to blame; my hopeful objective is to inspire racial healing between Blacks and racist Whites.

This is 2022, and the truth is that former President Trump did say something true about the "Charlottesville" encounter between racist Whites and antiracist folk.

President Trump stated that there were "good people on both sides." Although he received a lot of backlash for the statement, I have to say I agree with President Trump, but I also have to say this: There are a lot of good racist White people who unfortunately have a disillusioned view of Blacks because they have been brainwashed with lies about Black people. Black people have not done anything to you. We are willing to let the past be the past, so your hate for Black people is unnecessary.

Call to Action

My request or "Call to Action" for anyone who has read "Hate Without a Cause," whether you are a White person or a Black person or any race of people, is as follows:

1. If you are or were a racist White person that hates/hated Black people and my book has made a positive impression on you:
a. Take one day at a time to show kindness to Blacks personally and systemically.
b. Don't be afraid to engage Black people the same way as you engage Whites.
c. Take one day at a time to tear down the "walls of hate" in your heart and as much as possible replace those unneeded walls of hate with bridges of decency and nonjudgmental respect for everyone, no matter their color, age, race, creed, or gender, and enjoy your life.

2. If you are a White person who isn't a racist, but where you live everyone and particularly family and friends are racist, then:
a. MOVE AWAY!
b. Stop looking for peer approval, especially if their belief system of who to love or hate is really not your belief system.

Finally, COVID-19 has shown all of us that tomorrow isn't promised to anyone. Do yourself a favor: live, love, and pursue "happiness." Don't waste your life missing out on possible friendships with Black people just because you have been lied to about Black people and wrongly taught or convinced to hate Black people, especially now that you know that your hate towards Black people is

HATE WITHOUT A CAUSE

Biography

Born Brian Keith McNorton in Los Angeles, CA, "Jam" (Jesus Always Mandatory) McNorton received his nickname playing his guitar and singing on the subways of New York City in 2005 during his eight month stay in the city.

In 1970 Jam's mother, Mamie Lee Hillstock, moved Jam and his brothers and sisters to Santa Maria, California when he was 7 years old. From a child, until he graduated high school, Jam was known as Keith Hillstock.

The Hillstock family was respected in Santa Maria as some of the best musicians. It wasn't until Jam joined the U.S. Air Force at the ripe old age of 17, that he saw his birth certificate for the first time. The birth certificate showed his last name as McNorton (his father's last name) thus Jam became Brian Keith McNorton.

Considered by many, as well as himself, as a psychologist without a degree. Jam believes that his greatest gift is his love for people. No matter what race, color, gender or transgender, Jam loves you!

As an activist for racial equality, Jam McNorton has written songs and now this book. The best summation of Jam's beliefs on the subject of race relations is realized in his quote, "There is only once race, the "Human Race," and the rainbow is necessary!"

Jam resides in South Sacramento, California.

Jam McNorton

Made in the USA
Middletown, DE
28 September 2022